The United States, Russia, Europe, and Security: How to Address the "Unfinished Business" of the Post–Cold War Era

The United States, Russia, Europe, and Security: How to Address the "Unfinished Business" of the Post–Cold War Era

By Isabelle François

Center for Transatlantic Security Studies
Institute for National Strategic Studies
Transatlantic Perspectives, No. 2

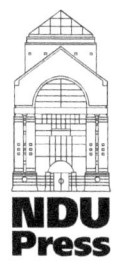

National Defense University Press
Washington, D.C.
April 2012

First printing, April 2012

For current publications of the Institute for National Strategic Studies, please go to the National Defense University Web site at: www.ndu.edu/inss.

Contents

Executive Summary

In 2012, the U.S. Department of Defense published *Sustaining U.S. Global Leadership: Priorities for 21st Century Defense.* In this strategy document, the Defense Department outlines the new focus of U.S. efforts on threats emanating primarily from South Asia and the Middle East, spelling out the U.S. commitment to address them by working with allies and partners, acknowledging Europe as the "home to some of America's most stalwart allies and partners." It clearly states that the United States "has enduring interests in supporting peace and prosperity in Europe as well as bolstering the strength and vitality of NATO [North Atlantic Treaty Organization], which is critical to the security of Europe and beyond." Moreover, the document characterizes engagement with Russia as important and reiterates U.S. commitment to continue efforts toward building a closer relationship in areas of mutual interest, encouraging Russia to be a contributor across a broad range of issues. The strategic environment will therefore remain one of partnership with Europe and Russia as nations work out the consequences of a rebalancing of forces in the near future.

In addition, the United States will be hosting the next NATO summit in Chicago on May 20–21, 2012. This will be an opportunity to send a strong message of Alliance solidarity in the face of budgetary restraints and will provide a concrete commitment to "smart defense" through pooling and sharing limited resources. The NATO summit might also provide an opportunity to consider what this means for NATO-Russia cooperation in an age of austerity. Immediately following Russian elections, there may be a case for reviewing the state of play between NATO and Russia, should the new Russian president seize the opportunity to refine his approach toward security cooperation with the West.

This paper, completed in February 2012, provides concrete ideas for the United States, Russia, and Europe to take account of the 2012 agenda, and refine their relationships toward the goal of partnership and the ultimate emergence of an inclusive European security community. The paper first provides an honest assessment of the NATO-Russia cooperation of the past 20 years and concludes that this relationship has yet to deliver a truly "strategic partnership" in line with the current rhetoric, many documents, and political declarations. It attempts to shed light on the Russian outlook and reviews the limits of the current partnership. It points to a significant level of "unfinished business" from the post–Cold War, which will have to be addressed if there is any hope of building a whole Europe that is free, undivided, and at peace.

The second part reviews the current challenges facing NATO Allies and Russia in three main areas: the reduction of nonstrategic nuclear weapons in Europe, stalemate regarding conventional forces in Europe, and limits of cooperation in missile defense. In reviewing the debate in these three areas, the paper offers options to move forward in each case but, in all three areas, concludes with the need for a broad political-military dialogue, reaching beyond the confines of the NATO-Russia relationship to broadly address Russian concerns. In each area, the paper points to fundamental disagreements that reach well beyond the issue at hand to a basic difference of views on the European security construct and on threat perceptions that ultimately reflect a fundamental lack of trust, paralyzing the strategic community.

The third and last part of the paper spells out a confidence-building program to reassure Russia regarding Western intentions and to develop trust through operational cooperation, transparency in contingency planning and exercising, dialogue about deterrence and transparency on safety measures regarding tactical nuclear weapons, smart defense approaches and projects, and possible joint installations and co-ownership as cooperation develops.

In conclusion, the paper argues for renewed bilateral and multilateral efforts toward a strategic partnership with Russia. It stresses, however, the requirement for a "confidence-building detour" on the road to an inclusive European security community. Today's agenda ought to focus on creating the conditions for this genuine strategic partnership to develop.

Introduction

Defining the best approach to engage Russia in today's political environment requires an ability to step back and consider a long-term strategic approach. Assuming the aim for the United States, Europe, and the North Atlantic Treaty Organization (NATO) remains to forge a "strategic partnership" with the Russian Federation, the exercise calls for a fresh look and a different approach. Indeed, the post–Cold War objective of creating a strategic partnership with Russia, albeit reaffirmed in all key NATO-Russia documents and most recent allied political statements, remains elusive, and the current European security environment speaks of a rather different relationship.

The first part of this paper briefly assesses the so-called strategic partnership forged between Allies and Russia over the past 20 years, and calls for addressing urgently the "unfinished business" in European security. Secondly, the paper considers the current challenges in engaging Russia on thorny issues, from nonstrategic nuclear weapons reduction and safety to the stalemate on conventional forces in Europe and the challenge of missile defense cooperation, to ultimately conclude that European security requires a broad and inclusive security dialogue where Russian concerns are both heard and addressed. The paper finally offers a set of concrete measures to build confidence and engage a broad political-military dialogue with Russia in an attempt to create the conditions to move forward on the long-term objective of cooperative security.

The paper deliberately focuses on the strategic level and bypasses the current challenge of getting through 2012, in terms of the recent Russian electoral process and popular unrest facing President Vladimir Putin, as well as the U.S. elections. These factors essentially preclude any significant breakthrough this year. Russia will only engage once the next U.S. President is elected. The paper, however, takes account of the 2012 Department of Defense *Sustaining U.S. Global Leadership: Priorities for 21ˢᵗ Century Defense*. While this strategy document outlines the new focus of U.S. efforts on threats perceived to emanate primarily from South Asia and the Middle East, it clearly spells out that when it comes to the U.S. Government's commitment to addressing these threats, it will do so by working with allies and partners. The document recognizes Europe as the "home to some of America's most stalwart allies and partners." In that context, the strategy states that the United States "has enduring interests in supporting peace and prosperity in Europe as well as bolstering the strength and vitality of NATO, which is critical to the security of Europe and beyond." Moreover, the Defense Department stresses its engagement with Russia as important, and commits to continued efforts to build a closer relationship in areas of mutual interest, encouraging Russia to be a contributor across a broad range of issues. The strategic environment will therefore remain one of partnership with Europe and Russia, even if some rebalancing of forces will be expected in the near future. It is in that context that the paper offers concrete ideas as the United States, Europe, and Russia proceed with a rebalancing of forces to create the conditions for cooperation to prevail.

Assessment of the NATO-Russia Strategic Partnership

A Relationship Based on False Premises

The NATO-Russia relationship was formally launched in 1997 when the Alliance and Russian Federation decided to create a forum for regular consultation on security issues—the Permanent Joint Council (PJC). The two sides seemed at the time to have decided to trade in an adversarial relationship based on escalating rhetoric, intimidation, and confrontation for one of dialogue and cooperation. The need for cooperation between the two camps had already been discussed with the dissolution of the Soviet Union in December 1991. President Boris Yeltsin at the time pledged Russia's participation in the North Atlantic Cooperation Council, and the Russian Federation even became a NATO partner in the mid-1990s when the Alliance created the Partnership for Peace, although the Russian military never fully engaged in that framework. Yeltsin ultimately suggested that Russia might someday become a NATO member, as he believed his country had more to gain from cooperation and engagement with NATO than from splendid isolation, running the risk of being excluded from the development of the 1990s and the reshaping of European security in the aftermath of the fall of the Berlin Wall.[1]

However, the relationship has also generated significant waves of disappointment and frustration over the past 20 years. The first major blow came in the wake of the Kosovo war in 1999, which prompted the Russians to suspend their ties with NATO. Yeltsin's approach to NATO at the time drew fierce criticism within Russia, especially from within the Duma (House of Representatives) and among military officers, who began articulating a long list of Russian resentments, including that NATO enlargement violated assurances that Russia received as part of the agreement to accept German unification.

When Lord George Islay Robertson, as NATO Secretary-General, and Putin met in October 2001 to reassess the potential for NATO-Russia relations after the Kosovo episode, they embarked on a new approach with a far-reaching multilateral process that would transform the NATO-Russia relationship and serve as a key instrument in anchoring Russia into a cooperative agenda with the West. In 2002, the Alliance and Russian Federation created the NATO-Russia

Council (NRC) to succeed the PJC and stressed that the new council would function as a forum of 20 *equal* members, avoiding the pitfalls of the previous forum, which had become essentially a confrontational environment opposing 19 Allies to 1 partner.[2]

In summer 2008, however, the Russo-Georgian conflict dealt a second major blow to the NATO-Russia construct. This time the Allies suspended the NRC and its activities, deciding that it could no longer be "business as usual" between NATO and Russia. For about a year, the NRC stopped holding meetings and cooperative activities came to a halt.

Many Allies believed that Russian actions in Georgia represented a serious challenge to the West. This belief—still lingering—was firmly anchored in the assumption that the conflict had been initiated by Russia and would have profound implications in strategic affairs resulting from an aggressive player seeking fundamental change to the existing international order. Others argued that the conflict with Georgia might have been simply exploited by Moscow using both military and diplomatic tools to send a strong message. Russia had felt for some time that it could no longer be the object of derision and accept the post–Cold War settlement, which was incompatible with its core national interests but had not been opposed by Moscow in the early 1990s owing to Russia's own weaknesses at the time.

Russian actions in Georgia were met with disappointment and disbelief on the part of the most moderate Allies, who were long supporters of NATO-Russia cooperation, but they served as justification for the Cold War warriors who called for punishment for what they perceived as an aggressive and anachronistic policy toward Russia's weak southern neighbor. Diverging interpretations of Russian actions in summer 2008 reinforced differences within the Alliance to a breaking point on how to best engage Moscow. The suspension of political dialogue and military cooperation between Russia and NATO resulted in polarized positions within the Alliance to this day, which has affected the normal functioning of the NRC and still hampers the development of an inclusive security community in Europe.

This polarization may have been rooted in a fundamental misunderstanding between NATO and Russia regarding their respective expectations, probably dating back to the onset of the relationship. NATO-Russia relations developed on the false premise that, on the one hand, Russia was on a path toward sharing and integrating Western values fundamental to the post–Cold War Alliance transformation. Russia was thereby perceived to be reconciled with NATO's "open door" policy in the 1990s. On the other hand, Russia believed that it was given a voice around the table in Euro-Atlantic security and could influence Alliance thinking from within. The creation of the NRC and the 2002 Rome Declaration were thus developed under the dubious assumption that all parties would be in a position to influence each other's decisionmaking processes and ensure a cooperative agenda in addressing common threats and challenges jointly.

Over the past decade, the ambitious 2002 NRC agenda has carefully evolved toward defining cooperation in "areas of common interest." It has become commonplace between NATO and Russia to "agree to disagree," recognizing that cooperation will be limited to areas where the parties can decide to work together, while on others they will work at cross-purposes. This amounts to revisiting the very concept of cooperative security and partnership, albeit tacitly. Russian authorities have nonetheless clearly stated that the prospect of NATO enlargement to Georgia and Ukraine presents a challenge to Russia's core national interests. In fact, their national documents, from their military doctrine to their foreign policy statements, have been unequivocal in this regard. Moreover, it is widely argued that the Russo-Georgian war was Moscow's attempt to put an end to any prospect of Georgia joining NATO.

Yet the resumption of NRC meetings and cooperation in the spring of 2009 proceeded on the same basis of partnership and cooperation as was developed in 1997 and 2002 on the understanding of agreeing to disagree in certain areas. In reality, the Alliance could not find the necessary consensus from within to refine the basis for its relationship with Russia, and it papered over the fact that various parties came out of the 2008–2009 period with different outlooks on the potential for the NATO-Russia relationship. The Russo-Georgian war should have been clearly identified as a turning point, where Moscow's objectives in using military force against Tbilisi marked a need felt in Moscow to delineate a Russian core national interest without necessarily sending a message of confrontation with the West. Recognizing the Russian position and taking it into account in the evolution of the NATO-Russia relationship, however, seemed impossible.

Instead, by the end of 2009, the NRC was back in business, at least on the surface. Looking at official documents issued on the occasion of the last NATO summit in November 2010, one discusses the importance that Allies attach to "developing a true strategic partnership between NATO and Russia," and of 29 NRC leaders pledging to "work towards achieving a true strategic and modernized partnership based on the principles of reciprocal confidence, transparency, and predictability, with the aim of contributing to the creation of a common space of peace, security and stability." Perhaps of most visible significance, the Lisbon Summit marked a renewed commitment to cooperation in the area of missile defense.[3]

For his part, the Secretary-General had already adopted that tone in September 2009 during his first major public speech in his NATO capacity, which was devoted entirely to NATO-Russia relations. He lamented that "We spend too much energy on what divides us. We should instead focus on what unites us." He did recognize, however, that NATO needed to "display greater realism" and acknowledged that "when the Cold War ended twenty years ago, NATO and Russia developed rather unrealistic expectations about each other—and those flawed expectations are still very much alive today and continue to burden our relationship." Most importantly, he admitted something rarely mentioned in the West: "that Russia has security interests which we need to understand and take into account. Many things that NATO Allies may regard as entirely benign can sometimes look very different when seen from Moscow—and vice versa."[4]

That said, for the past 2 years, the Secretary-General has often been ahead of the Allies in his approach to NATO-Russia cooperation and ahead of consensus, as his leadership role might have required. However, in the last few months, allied consensus and the political reality of Russian internal debates, especially in the runup to the 2012 elections, have brought a new form of realism to the fore. In a statement on missile defense, on November 23, 2011, the Secretary-General felt obliged to officially "take note of President [Dmitriy] Medvedev's statement on missile defense" and to express that "[Medvedev's] suggestion that the [Russian] deployment of missiles in the areas neighboring the Alliance is an appropriate response to NATO's system is very disappointing."[5]

In reality, behind the Lisbon rhetoric and just below the surface lies an uneasy partnership between NATO and Russia still suffering from the impact of the Russo-Georgian war. This conflict called into question the core assumption binding NATO and Russia into a partnership, namely that Russia would become progressively more integrated into the Western community of states. Events and declarations in the last 5 years have often diverged from the cooperative agenda of the 1997 Founding Act and 2002 Rome Declaration, highlighting a more competitive and, at times, even confrontational relationship. In fact, 20 years of NATO-Russia cooperation have evolved to the point where the so-called strategic partnership is of limited impact in addressing current strategic issues in Europe and beyond, and has become a liability within NATO regarding Alliance consensus-building. The NRC has not been able to develop a European security framework where all 29 members believe that their respective interests are equally addressed, and it has accordingly failed in developing an inclusive security community within Europe.

The NATO-Russia relationship has become often contentious, thus falling short of the positive and ambitious intentions enshrined in the key documents governing it. The relationship remains based on two key documents that hardly reflect the state of it but that remain central to the ultimate goal of cooperative security. The Founding Act on Mutual Relations, Cooperation, and Security (1997) continues to provide key principles, which will remain useful in guiding the relationship toward transparency, reciprocity, and predictability.[6] The document also has the merit of being widely recognized as a basis for the relationship both in Moscow and within the Alliance. The Rome Declaration (2002) for its part has served as a solid basis for an ambitious cooperative framework for a NATO-Russia relationship but may seem overly optimistic today.[7] It hardly reflects the current state of affairs between NATO and Russia. It remains, nonetheless, one of the founding documents and continues to anchor the whole structure developed toward cooperation.

In the current strategic environment, however, it is not entirely clear whether NATO-Russia relations should be best framed solely within a win-win cooperative agenda. As the NATO Secretary-General acknowledged in September 2009: "Yes we found great language for our partnership aims in the NATO-Russia Founding Act and the Rome Declaration—but we have not been able to translate them into reality. Yes we cooperated on a number of issues—but this cooperation was always kept hostage to the overall political climate. One major disagreement and it would falter."[8] The fact is that what was true in September 2009 and up to that point is still true today. Moreover, it might be useful to refine the NATO-Russia agenda to account for what may only be a "transition period" toward the long-term goal of cooperative security, thus acknowledging that there is unfinished business that will require effort and attention to ensure that the relationship remains on the cooperative security track and avoid bifurcation in European security.

Insights into the Russian Outlook

The events of summer 2008 were a watershed in NATO-Russia relations, and they revealed fundamental differences in allied and Russian strategic cultures and the respective articulation of foreign policy objectives. In advancing foreign policy objectives, Russian leaders are operating within a strategic culture markedly different from the value-based approach that predominates within the Western community of liberal democracies. Foreign policy under both Putin and Medvedev has been aimed at creating a favorable environment for economic and sociopolitical modernization, while ensuring that Russia is not weakened on the international scene. Many Russians have not reconciled themselves to the loss both of international status and of Russian identity that resulted from the collapse of the Soviet Union and its empire. As a result, Putin's Russia has been predominantly influenced by a desire to build a "strong state" and a more assertive foreign policy. The construction of Russia's political identity is still under development, and, therefore, its foreign policy and the use of force within this context seem to assist in developing a policy of "national recovery." In that sense, the national dimension within Russia of debates around international issues has a fundamental importance for the leadership. In many ways, NATO-Russia relations have often become hostage to domestic politics in Russia—usually to a greater extent than in allied countries, where it is simply a matter of different political platforms within a democratic system.

In addition, most Western liberal democracies see the use of armed forces as a last resort and diplomacy as the art of avoiding crises. In Russia, the use of armed forces is very much an instrument of foreign policy, and, as demonstrated in summer 2008, it is considered a legitimate and useful means to assert strategic goals. Russian posturing, therefore, should not necessarily be construed as the beginning of a new period of confrontation with the West, let alone a return to the Cold War era. Nonetheless, in 2008, possible misinterpretation that the events signaled a direct military confrontation with the United States and its Allies could have led to an incalculable escalation of tensions, and remains a liability in Western relations with Russia.[9]

Furthermore, the Allies' approach to conflicts lies in the art of consensus and diplomatic efforts toward resolving differences through peaceful means. Russian diplomacy, by contrast, borrows heavily from its imperial foreign policy tradition and might seek out or exploit crises to advance strategic goals tactically. As a result, confrontation or simple competition often coexists with cooperation. One could usefully consider the debates over Putin's December 2007 suspension of the Conventional Armed Forces in Europe (CFE) Treaty as a means to increase tensions. Similarly, Russia's disagreements with NATO and the United States over missile defense, usually amplified by harsh and perhaps threatening rhetoric, have often aimed at raising tensions to ultimately exploit opportunities. As tensions decrease, the Russian leadership usually welcomes efforts to bridge the divisions between the parties and to work more cooperatively. It would seem pointless, however, to expect Russia to choose between confrontation, competition, or cooperation. The combination is a must in managing its foreign policy. Western expectations regarding coherence between policy and public declarations by Russian officials or even among Russian officials are misplaced.

Moreover, misunderstanding and unavoidable disappointment with Russian foreign policy seem more rooted in exaggerated allied expectations regarding the speed of its modernization than in its foreign policy inconsistencies. Despite its natural resources and frequent evidence of a new self-confidence—not to say aggressive posturing—Russian leadership knows that the country is weak. While the Western style would likely lead to a less visible stand in foreign policy in the case of similar weakness, Russian strategic culture begs for a more aggressive tone in the face of its own vulnerability. The country is facing considerable economic and demographic challenges and is highly unlikely to endanger its relations with the West.

Finally, Moscow does recognize that there is no real challenge to American global leadership, although tensions between the United States and Europe and various transatlantic disputes will be considered as useful constraints on Washington, and potentially useful tensions to be exploited by a Russian leadership mastering the art of playing a weak hand. Ultimately, Russia often faces a choice between focusing its relations with the West on the bilateral relationship with the United States, exploiting the refocusing of American power away from Europe, and playing on differences within Europe to challenge the post–Cold War system. Consistent with its traditional approach, Russia will likely waiver and play different hands, at times focusing on the bilateral relationship with Washington and then returning to multilateralism, siding with others when its own national interests dictate.

Preeminence of the Bilateral Relationships and Limits of the Multilateral Frameworks

In 2007, during the last visit of previous NATO Secretary-General Jaap de Hoop Scheffer to Moscow, President Putin wondered aloud whether Russian interest was likely to be best served by focusing its foreign policy on the bilateral relationship with the United States or by playing the multilateral card in the face of what was then a perceived ebbing of American power. With hindsight, the Russian choice was clearly made in favor of bilateral relations.

The difficulty in anchoring Russia into a multilateral cooperative game also lies in the already mentioned differences among the Allies in their approach toward Russia, also evident within the European Union (EU). These divisions have been reinforced during the Russo-Georgian conflict, but were already captured by the unfortunate terminology coined by former U.S. Defense Secretary Donald Rumsfeld pitting "old Europe" against "new Europe," thereby differentiating between longstanding members of the Alliance and those who recently joined, allowing new members to escape from the inescapable history of belonging to the Soviet bloc. The divisions are perhaps more complex if one considers the Canadian position, often aligned with "new Europeans." Indeed Canada, Poland, the Baltic States, the Czech Republic, and Great Britain advocated a strong response to the war, including the suspension of security cooperation with Moscow. Others such as France, Italy, and Germany urged the Alliance to avoid any escalation of tensions. This episode demonstrated the challenge of designing a common approach to Russia and has often paralyzed the Alliance in its relations with this so-called strategic partner.

Allies who have the most invested, politically and financially, in a solid bilateral relationship with Moscow, and who have benefited from a longstanding tradition of close relations with Russia, can ill-afford to alienate Moscow multilaterally, and certainly have no intention of abandoning their policies of engagement. In fact, judging from the position of the EU, none of the European states seems ready for political confrontation with Moscow in a multilateral framework, and this cannot have escaped Moscow. Any attempt at realpolitik with Russia on the part of the EU or NATO would be both shortsighted and likely short term. Divisions among Allies still exist and in fact present opportunities to be exploited by Moscow. Russian leadership, often seen as pragmatic, will continue to exploit any advantage it can find in a fluid and dynamic international environment, and, as a weaker player, Russia will take advantage of the real or perceived vulnerabilities of its stronger opponents.

In the last few years, Moscow has favored bilateral relations with key Allies over multilateralism, given the challenges facing both the NATO-Russia relationship and the EU-Russia dynamic. First among equals, the U.S.-Russia bilateral relationship remains central to Russia's engagement with the West. While U.S. global leadership is challenging to Russian authorities favoring a polycentric international order, Moscow is still prepared to accept the United States *primus inter pares* to the extent that this status is fully consistent in Washington with reciprocal respect and recognition of respective national interests. Moscow is not necessarily different in its approach to U.S. leadership than some other European powers, and the Russian temptation to align with these like-minded capitals remains a permanent fixture of what Moscow perceives to be a fluid and competitive international environment.

Quite apart from Russian criticism of what is perceived as American unilateralism, Moscow believes Washington to be inimical to its recovery and harbors considerable distrust of American intentions. Russians have long assessed Washington's discourse on values and democratization as fundamentally disingenuous, with the sole purpose of serving global expansion. By extension, the whole partnership and cooperation agenda over the past 20 years at NATO is viewed with great skepticism in Moscow.

When taking office, Barack Obama made an early signal of his wish for improved relations with Russia and focused on the reduction of nuclear arms as an obvious shared concern that could yield early results. In July 2009, Presidents Obama and Medvedev were able to reach a framework agreement to cut their strategic nuclear arsenals by a third. The New Strategic Arms Reduction Treaty (New START) was signed and ratified in 2011. That said, the new treaty did not eliminate a host of vexing issues in the U.S.-Russia relationship, but it took the relationship a significant step forward and served as the basis for the U.S. "reset" policy toward Russia.

Similarly, some positive momentum in U.S.-Russia relations on missile defense during the same period did not mean that grievances in this area had disappeared, especially given the level of anti-Americanism within Russian politics. However, the Kremlin had taken the hard edge off U.S.-Russia relations during the reset period and directed the media to cut the negative references to the United States. With the 2012 electoral processes under way both in Moscow and in Washington, the lull came to an end, and the future of the reset policy is now on the table. This will considerably affect the NATO-Russia relationship and the prospects for an NRC summit in Chicago in May 2012. As the NATO Secretary-General stated in his famous 2009 speech on NATO-Russia, "I am also keenly aware that NATO-Russia relations can quickly become hostage to domestic politics—in Russia as well as in allied nations. After all, the state of NATO-Russia relations is very much a reflection of the state of bilateral relations between individual Allies and Russia."[10] The bilateral U.S.-Russia and the multilateral relationship between NATO and Russia have never been so closely intertwined, so key security issues on the Chicago Summit agenda will be closely affected by the evolution of the reset policy.

Current Challenges: From Arms Control to Cooperative Security

Follow-on to New START and NATO Deterrence and Defense Posture Review

When President Obama signed the New START, he committed to follow-on negotiations with the Russian Federation to address reductions in nonstrategic and nondeployed strategic nuclear warheads. In his February 2, 2011, letter to the Senate, he stated that "The U.S. will seek to initiate, following consultation with NATO allies, but no later than one year after the entry into force of New START, negotiations with the Russian Federation on an agreement to address the disparity between the nonstrategic (tactical) nuclear weapons stockpiles of the Russian Federation and of the United States and to secure and reduce tactical nuclear weapons in a verifiable manner." In parallel, a couple of months earlier, the 2010 NATO Lisbon Summit Declaration, issued by allied heads of state and government, asked the North Atlantic Council "to continue to review NATO's overall posture in deterring and defending against the full range of threats to the Alliance, taking into account changes in the evolving international security environment." It further clarified that "Essential elements of the review would include the range of NATO's strategic capabilities required, including NATO's nuclear posture, and missile defense and other means of strategic deterrence and defense."[11] To that end, the NATO Deterrence and Defense Posture Review (DDPR) was launched in 2011 with the aim of reporting to heads of state and government at the Chicago Summit in 2012.

Both sets of discussions are effectively focusing on nonstrategic nuclear weapons and more specifically, nonstrategic weapons deployed in Europe. American officials have recognized the importance of consulting with NATO Allies as they develop their approach to negotiations with Russia. Some U.S. officials are pushing forward to build on the momentum of New START, while others see less urgency given the lack of consensus and the difficult debate within NATO, but also given the lack of Russian interest in early negotiations. In light of the DDPR debate, there would seem to be little room for negotiations in terms of U.S. nonstrategic nuclear weapons deployed in Europe, and therefore little hope of initiating negotiations with the Russian Federation on its nonstrategic nuclear weapons stockpiles in the near term, especially in 2012, an election year in the United States, Russian Federation, and France. There may yet be some options for establishing confidence-building and transparency measures with Russia regarding nonstrategic nuclear weapons either bilaterally or multilaterally.

A Difficult Political Context. In the framework of the 2010 Lisbon Summit and the new NATO Strategic Concept, the United States and its Allies had managed a damaging internal debate in the face of their diverging views on nuclear issues. Most will be reluctant to go beyond the Lisbon Compromise for fear of reopening the discussions and feeding into a delicate public debate. The Allies agreed on a carefully crafted position that reflected both President Obama's Prague agenda—reducing the number and role of nuclear weapons—and the five principles articulated by Secretary of State Hillary Clinton at the informal NATO ministerial in Tallinn, Estonia, in April 2010.[12] These principles informed the development of the new NATO Strategic Concept and seemed to have reassured the Central and Eastern European Allies, who had originally reacted vehemently against any possible change in Alliance nuclear policy. The principles also helped in managing the significant differences between the French and German positions on nuclear issues.

That said, consensus in the runup to the Lisbon Summit was held up until the very last hours of summit preparations on three issues, which were deemed interrelated by one nation: NATO's nuclear policy, missile defense, and NATO-Russia relations.[13] The fact that this paper is addressing all three issues is not a coincidence, as these fundamental issues are indeed related and remain essentially unresolved despite language agreement in Lisbon. Far from being reconciled, diverging views regarding NATO's nuclear policy remain below the surface, compounded by significant differences on the way to engage with Russia, notably on the thorny issue of missile defense cooperation.

In today's enlarged NATO, Allies no longer share the same understanding of risks and threats. While the countries of Central and Eastern Europe still fear the perceived threat of Russia, the countries of Western and Southern Europe are more focused on new security challenges. Some have characterized the debate as a controversy between the "enlightened disarmers" who follow President Obama's call for nuclear disarmament—with Germany as the most vocal representative of the group—and the "Cold War warriors" of Central and Eastern Europe, quietly backed by Turkey and also supported by France for different reasons. This is, however, an oversimplification of the current debate. In fact, the compromise—developed around the

Strategic Concept that will prevail in the course of the DDPR exercise—is one of compromise, which is certainly a disappointment to the proponents of an early withdrawal, but which safeguards consensus with a solution pushing for gradual change rather than a revolution.

On the other hand, there is a growing recognition that in the midterm, it will no longer be possible to continue with nuclear "business as usual," and this will most likely resurface in the wake of upcoming American cuts in Europe. Of course, many will argue that the United States and NATO should not make unilateral decisions based on the previous wave of disarmament enthusiasm, but rather approach the issue of reduction of nonstrategic nuclear weapons in Europe in a holistic manner. This would call for a serious attempt to engage with Russia, which stores nonstrategic nuclear weapons on the European part of its territory, and in much greater numbers than the United States does.

Over time, the question will likely evolve from *whether* to *how* to proceed with reductions of nuclear weapons in Europe. In fact, Poland joined Norway to offer a set of proposals aimed at addressing the issue of substrategic nuclear weapons in a larger framework of European arms control issues. The joint communiqué from the April 2010 meeting of the Polish and Norwegian foreign ministers suggested a "step-by-step approach, including transparency and confidence-building measures as well as balanced and mutual arms reductions." Similarly, an op-ed by the Polish and Swedish foreign ministers published in the *New York Times* called for moving the NATO internal debate into the NATO-Russia agenda addressing nuclear weapons in Europe as "dangerous remnants of a dangerous past."[14]

Toward a Carefully Balanced Approach within NATO. The timing is crucial, however, and 2012 with its electoral "rendezvous" may not be opportune. Nonetheless, there is a need to start working on a carefully balanced approach between polarized positions, with a step-by-step solution evolving over time. This solution will require a Russian dimension. The development of a holistic approach begs for urgently engaging Moscow with an offer to discuss the ultimate withdrawal of all substrategic nuclear weapons from Europe as part of an overall framework for dealing with both offensive and defensive systems and nuclear and nonnuclear deterrence capabilities, reflecting on the original DDPR exercise, which called on the Alliance to define the appropriate mix of conventional, nuclear, and missile defense forces in Europe for its deterrence and defense posture.

At the Chicago Summit, however, a message of continuity will be fundamental to safeguard consensus and cater to the much-needed message of solidarity within the Alliance in times of fiscal constraint, and also in light of U.S. defense cuts in Europe. Continuity should not preclude movement in order to slowly gear the Alliance toward a deliberate adaptation of its nuclear posture, especially as elements of change have already taken root. Indeed, the Allies have first agreed in the 2010 Strategic Concept that the objectives of deterrence and arms control can be pursued together. The ultimate goal is the pursuit of deterrence, nonproliferation, and arms control in the context of a vision of a nuclear-free world. The second element of change lies in the overall NATO approach of defining the appropriate mix of conventional, nuclear, and missile defense forces by looking at the deterrence and defense posture in a holistic fashion. The third element of change stems from the Allies having agreed that future reductions in U.S. nuclear forces in Europe must involve Russian reciprocity. This does imply a new situation whereby U.S. nuclear force reductions now depend on Russia and its interest in further arms control negotiations.

How Best to Engage Russia? Following the Lisbon Summit, and in line with the five principles outlined by Secretary Clinton, most officials and diplomats concede today that the summit de facto created a linkage between changes in NATO's nuclear posture and an agreement with Russia on the reduction of its stockpile of tactical nuclear weapons. There are still some who argue that NATO members in Lisbon did not establish Russian reciprocity as a direct and explicit precondition for future changes of NATO's nuclear posture, but, in the end, one can safely say that there is at minimum a constructive ambiguity.

Russia is believed to have around 2,000 operational tactical nuclear weapons and thousands more in various states of readiness.[15] Others specify that it would have 3,700 to 5,400 nonstrategic nuclear warheads of all types, with a deliverable capacity of about 2,000.[16] The new Strategic Concept states that "any further steps" to reduce nuclear weapons in Europe "must take into account the disparity with the greater Russian stockpiles of short-range nuclear weapons." It also states that "In any future reductions, NATO's aim should be to seek Russian agreement to increase transparency on its nuclear weapons in Europe and relocate these weapons away from the territory of NATO members." So the greater number of Russian tactical nuclear weapons is effectively one element that NATO will have to factor in when reviewing its nuclear posture. While the disparities between stockpiles may remain for the time being, there is at least an element of reciprocity in requiring Russian movement on transparency.

The Lisbon Summit Declaration indicated that the NRC should be the venue to discuss "the overall disparity in short-range nuclear weapons," although this has yet to be agreed to by the Russian side. The Strategic Concept was even more ambitious addressing the whole arms control, disarmament, and nonproliferation agenda, and the Allies agreed to create a new committee to that end. However, no one in NATO has yet engaged the Russians on any of these issues formally, while discussions among Allies are ongoing in the context of DDPR.

Washington sees a possibility of reducing U.S. nuclear weapons in Europe, but in considering its position, it will want to reassure Central and Eastern European Allies and be mindful that nuclear policy in Europe has global implications. Any U.S. proposal for negotiations on nonstrategic nuclear weapons with Russia will therefore be vetted with the Allies. While the Obama administration does not regard Russia as a threat and does not see a need for the DDPR to strengthen deterrence against Russia, U.S. officials are mindful of the concerns of Central and Eastern European Allies for whom the U.S. nuclear umbrella now seems to play a more important role than for other Allies. This approach has so far made it largely impossible to engage with Russia in the NRC on its forward deployed substrategic systems, given the differences among Allies on how to engage Russia in these talks.

For all the challenges in maintaining consensus within the Alliance, the wild card is actually the Russia card, that is, whether and how soon the Russians will be ready for further negotiations. The current signals coming out of Moscow suggest that they are in no hurry. Negotiations thus will not prove easy. There are several reasons. First, the number of Russian tactical nuclear weapons is significantly higher than that of the active U.S. forces or stockpiles. This would basically lead to an asymmetrical accord where Russian reductions would be required, and perhaps only Russian reductions. It is acknowledged as largely impossible to get Moscow to agree to anything other than "equal limits" through negotiations. The likelihood of a zero/zero option, eliminating all nonstrategic nuclear warheads on both sides, is no more likely. According to some American analysts, the only viable option would seem to include nonstrategic warheads with other nuclear weapons limits. The option of a single limit might be appealing to the Russians who, for their part, would be interested in capping the number of U.S. nondeployed strategic warheads—an area of U.S. advantage. This might actually be the only incentive for the Russians to engage in reductions of their nonstrategic weapons.[17]

Second, the Russians assign their tactical nuclear weapons greater strategic importance in offsetting conventional weakness and deterring future threats from their south and east. When it comes to Russian conventional weakness vis-à-vis the Alliance, it may be noted that declining defense budgets will result in Allies shedding rather than adding conventional capabilities, making it difficult for conventional forces to assume a greater share of the load in the mix with nuclear and missile defense forces. Moreover, ongoing attempts to revive negotiations on conventional forces in Europe could provide additional reassurance to Russia and some incentives and a mechanism to approach possible reductions in nonstrategic nuclear weapons. It should be noted, however, that CFE will not address other Russian perceived threats from the south and the east.

Third, there are also competitive political stakes in Moscow's position. Official Russian statements have explicitly tied drawdown in tactical weapons to a general geopolitical rebalancing, given U.S. conventional superiority and the ongoing Russian opposition to NATO enlargement past and future. The Russians have also stated that they will not consider reducing their tactical nuclear stockpile until all U.S. weapons are removed from European territory. As a principle, they have essentially declared that all tactical weapons should be based on national territories of nuclear weapons states. In that context, there will be a need to engage in a broad dialogue with Russia on strategic issues, including the ultimate withdrawal of all substrategic nuclear weapons from Europe as the endgame rather than a precondition, with interim transparency and confidence-building measures to trigger Russian interest and jumpstart the process.

More controversial seems to be the issue of embedding any change of NATO's nuclear posture in an arms control agreement with Russia. Some argue that a strong linkage between changes of NATO's future nuclear posture and Moscow's nuclear policy is both unneeded and counterproductive. It is unneeded because there no longer exists a strategic connection between the tactical nuclear postures of NATO and Russia. This has been a constant in the last key policy documents and statements of the Alliance. These weapons may be included in future arms control talks, but there should remain a degree of autonomy for the Alliance to decide on its nuclear posture. By putting these weapons directly in an arms control context, NATO would be putting itself pretty much at the mercy of Moscow in terms of any changes it may wish to initiate on its nuclear posture.[18]

A Possible Way Ahead. As mentioned, a crucial step in addressing the issues raised by tactical nuclear weapons will be to build consensus among Allies and agree with Russia on total transparency, verification, and the right to monitor changes and movement of the arsenals. As specified in the Strategic Concept, greater transparency regarding Russian nonstrategic nuclear forces in Europe and relocation of those forces away from NATO borders will be important. It is worth mentioning that the Russians are believed to have substrategic nuclear weapons on their northwestern borders (of most concern to Allies) and in the Far East, given Chinese conventional superiority. Notably, relocation of tactical weapons away from the northwest borders into mainland Russia is not a message that will appeal to Russia's eastern neighbors, and this might create a new set of issues beyond the scope of this paper.

The real issue for the United States, NATO, and Russia is to what extent the Alliance can increase transparency and confidence-building with Russia without weakening its deterrence and defense posture. Tactical nuclear weapons have never been included in any arms control or disarmament treaties and the process is still undefined. Moreover, consensus within NATO on nuclear issues is currently challenged in the context of DDPR, and most of the issues that would have to be discussed with Russia are classified. It is hardly conceivable that the Allies could come to an agreement on transparency vis-à-vis Russia on allied nuclear posture. What is conceivable from NATO's perspective (and supported by some) is an exchange of information on inventories, stockpiles, and the eventual movement of these weapons, setting up a verification process to that end. Increasing transparency on the numbers, locations, and types of nonstrategic forces in Europe could be a first step.

Some Allies believe that possible changes to NATO's nuclear posture may be a bargaining chip to engage the Russians in reductions of tactical nuclear weapons. However, negotiating reductions multilaterally with Russia may not be the best approach as it would lock NATO's flexibility in terms of its posture and limit possible unilateral reductions or adaptations in the future. Moreover, the asymmetry between the numbers on the Russian and NATO sides would not easily yield to negotiations. Reductions on the one hand, and transparency and verification on the other, would be best addressed separately.

Reductions could be pursued in the bilateral U.S.-Russia New START follow-on negotiations, taking full account of the current consultations among Allies within the DDPR exercise, while contributions to confidence-building, transparency, and openness measures could be pursued multilaterally. Moreover, the consultations to take place multilaterally could be issue-based on specific dimensions of transparency and confidence-building. For instance, greater transparency regarding doctrine might be a way to start, as many in the West find it hard to understand why Russia maintains such a significant inventory of tactical nuclear weapons. Similarly, Russia has little faith in NATO doctrine, so greater transparency could benefit all sides.

Verification will present a major issue—that of monitoring challenges—in any negotiations covering nonstrategic nuclear weapons. Again, one may have to consider a bilateral approach (U.S.-Russia) to develop a verification system in the context of New START follow-on negotiations, and pursue confidence-building through a consolidation of weapons at a few storage sites, and relocation of tactical nuclear weapons on the Russian side away from the NATO-Russia borders. This may also be accomplished within a renewed CFE Treaty framework, which in time could allow tactical nuclear weapons to be subject to types and rates of inspections similar to those the CFE Treaty establishes for conventional weapons. Ultimately, one may not have to choose between the bilateral (U.S.-Russia) and the multilateral (NATO-Russia) approaches, and one might actually combine them.

The Russian position remains a challenge, as Minister Sergey Lavrov reiterated at an NRC ministerial meeting in Berlin last year, because Moscow is reluctant to engage on tactical nuclear weapons. The Kremlin has previously linked the issue to reassurances on missile defense. The Russians also link consultation on tactical nuclear weapons to progress on CFE issues, and progress would have to be forthcoming in the runup to the summit. Chicago may actually offer an opportunity to initiate a broad dialogue, as called for by Lavrov, who clearly stated that reductions in tactical nuclear weapons can only be achieved as part of a multinational (rather than bilateral) accord limiting other types of armaments such as conventional forces. There is always the possibility of agreeing to an NRC meeting of foreign ministers in Chicago, should President Putin choose to focus on the G8 meeting in Camp David.

However, NATO may yet have to acknowledge that until there is meaningful progress with Russia in terms of overall strategic dialogue on European security, there is little that will be achieved in the nonstrategic nuclear weapons debate, and U.S. nuclear weapons will have to stay in Europe. Russia will rely on nuclear weapons to compensate for the imbalance as long as it perceives a conventional superiority of NATO forces in Europe. Only when this Russian perception is assuaged will it be possible to find a solution regarding the status of tactical nuclear weapons in Europe. Dealing with these threat perceptions will require finding ways to develop a security architecture that can deter today's threats in a different way, more akin to the vision agreed to at the Rome Summit in 2002 where the NRC was established. In many ways today, the task for the Allies is not only to provide internal reassurances, but also to consider reassuring Russia by developing a constructive dialogue with Moscow over European security issues.

Stalemate over Conventional Forces in Europe

Signed in 1990, the CFE Treaty enabled NATO and the Warsaw Pact to stabilize their military relations by agreeing to destroy tens of thousands of pieces of military equipment and provide a climate of transparency unprecedented during the Cold War. However, with the end of the Warsaw Pact and collapse of the Soviet Union, the CFE Treaty was quickly overtaken by events. In addition, NATO enlargement and NATO-Russia cooperation were going to alter the European security landscape to such an extent that CFE member states soon began negotiating an adapted CFE Treaty, which was signed in 1999. However, the adapted treaty was never ratified by the Allies. Russia, for its part, as one of the few members to ratify this adapted version, failed to fulfill side commitments entered into as part of the 1999 adapted treaty negotiations. In December 2007, Moscow announced that it was "suspending" its observance of the original treaty. The CFE Treaty regime remains in limbo.

The CFE Treaty, considered by many as the cornerstone of European security, is on the verge of collapse, thus creating significant uncertainty regarding the intentions of various

European countries and reducing transparency in the movement of military forces in Europe. Serious efforts have been made since 2007 to bridge the divide, but the standoff continues. As mentioned, in the absence of a functioning CFE regime, there is concern that Russia will increase its reliance on tactical nuclear weapons to defend itself from what Moscow now sees as NATO's conventional superiority in Europe. This, in turn, will make the Obama administration's desire to tackle the challenge of reducing tactical nuclear weapons more difficult. Reengaging on CFE is therefore part and parcel of the overall debate on the U.S.-Russia arms control approach and core to the U.S. reset policy vis-à-vis Russia. It is also a significant piece of the puzzle for making real progress on NATO-Russia cooperation.

Signed on November 19, 1990, the CFE Treaty, negotiated during the final years of the Cold War, effectively eliminated the Soviet Union's overwhelming quantitative advantage in conventional weapons in Europe by setting equal limits on the number of tanks, armored combat vehicles, heavy artillery, combat aircraft, and attack helicopters that NATO and the Warsaw Pact could deploy between the Atlantic Ocean and the Ural Mountains.

The CFE Treaty's original goal was to prevent either alliance from amassing forces for a surprise offensive, which might have triggered the use of nuclear weapons in response. There has indeed always been a link between conventional and nuclear forces. Ironically, the Cold War picture is in many ways a mirror image in reverse of today's environment. In 1990, for the United States and NATO, the CFE Treaty allowed the Alliance to address the dangers of an overwhelming Soviet Union with its Warsaw Pact superiority in conventional weapons in Europe. This superiority meant that NATO would have had to resort to nuclear weapons to win a war in case of deterioration of the Cold War. Today, the situation is one of conventional inferiority in Europe on the Russian side, which may prompt Moscow to resort to nuclear weapons in case of war, or at least to increase its reliance on tactical nuclear weapons. The United States and its Allies are therefore attempting to reengage with Russia, but they will have to address the imbalance in terms of conventional weapons, if not before at least in parallel with any attempt to negotiate a reduction of tactical nuclear weapons.

In 2002, when Moscow declared that it had met the adapted treaty's weapons limits, NATO accepted the claim but reminded Russia of its commitments regarding Georgia and Moldova and indicated that ratification of the adapted CFE Treaty would be conditional upon the fulfillment of these commitments. The adapted treaty was only to enter into force when all 30 states parties had ratified the agreement. Only Belarus, Kazakhstan, Russia, and Ukraine have ratified so far. As a result, the original treaty is the one currently in effect. One of the additional complications with the ratification process pending is that four new NATO members (Estonia,

Latvia, Lithuania, and Slovenia) were not party to the original treaty and have no arms limits. Moreover, no provision exists for additional countries to accede to the original treaty; they must wait to join the adapted treaty once it enters into force.

Prior to the 2008 Georgia-Russia conflict, Russia had withdrawn from, and closed, three of the four bases in Georgia, but remained in Gudauta. Fifty-eight trainloads of equipment and ammunition had also been removed from Trandniestria by 2004. Citing the ongoing delay of the adapted treaty's entry into force, Russia issued a statement on December 12, 2007, suspending its implementation of the CFE Treaty (bearing in mind that the treaty does not contain a provision for suspension, only for withdrawal). Under suspension, Moscow stated that it would not participate in treaty data exchanges, notifications, or inspections. Although the Kremlin noted that it had no plans for arms buildups, it declared that it would not be bound by treaty limits. NATO members, including the United States, called on Russia to reverse course and declared their intention to continue implementing the treaty "without prejudice to any future action they might take."[19]

Shall We Fight for CFE? Given the current stalemate, one may wonder whether the CFE Treaty still serves a purpose. Many argue that it has little relevance today, while acknowledging that it played an important role in the Cold War and was a key tool in the immediate post–Cold War environment as a stabilization factor in the face of the collapse of the Warsaw Pact and Soviet Union. Nowadays, however, no national power or coalition has the conventional force capacity to wage the large-scale war against which the CFE Treaty was conceived. Given today's fiscal environment, that capacity is unlikely to develop in the next decade. Moreover, for the United States and its Allies, who enjoy conventional superiority, there would seem to be little incentive to spend political capital to revive the treaty. In fact, current NATO states parties are well below their current national ceilings imposed by the treaty, and the Russian army, which has recovered somewhat from its weakened condition of a decade ago, is still far from a strategic threat to NATO. Moscow is also confronted with budgetary choices in modernizing its strategic nuclear forces, navy, and army. Experts agree that the Russian army is at least a decade away from developing a capability to pose a large-scale conventional threat in Europe. Moreover, Russia is likely to be more concerned with its capabilities in the Far East and the growing size and sophistication of Chinese conventional forces.

That said, the CFE Treaty has contributed to a regime of transparency and limitation, which is still relevant in today's uncertain European security environment, especially on the eastern edge of NATO. While the environment is not one of direct threat to the Alliance, it still has the potential of becoming a zone of instability and heightened suspicions, which in turn could reverse favorable trends in Europe. CFE limitations on overall levels of forces and the transparency of confidence- and security-building measures (CSBMs) on military activities remain a valuable instrument of regulation of military forces and a regulator of behavior, respectively, binding those in the West who feel relatively secure with those in the East who have been increasingly anxious about Russian saber-rattling. That said, the CFE regime certainly did not prevent Russian exploitation of the crisis in Georgia in 2008. Interestingly enough, during the conflict, the limitations on military forces were respected, so one might question the value added by CFE in terms of conflict prevention as well as conflict resolution.

Irrespective of CFE's impact on conflict prevention and resolution, its disappearance would likely feed into a deeper division of Europe into two security zones: a relatively secure Western zone and a less secure Eastern zone, which would in turn exacerbate East-West relations. CFE, along with the parallel CSBMs regime, play an important political security role as a source of reassurance to address the concerns of Russia's neighbors. For CFE states on Russia's periphery—Georgia, Armenia, Azerbaijan, Moldova, and Ukraine—CFE allows for monitoring their neighbors. In principle, it is also an element of transparency and therefore reassurance for Russia, and certainly provides to all an opportunity to have a voice at the table with NATO countries and within the CFE Joint Consultative Group.

Indeed, Russia benefitted from transparency regarding NATO forces including those operating on the territory of newest NATO members who are CFE parties—both in terms of their own equipment and equipment stationed permanently on their territories. CFE in that sense could mitigate Russia's concerns over NATO deployment of military infrastructure close to its borders. Moreover, effective limits in Europe could only help the Russian military, which may have continued to benefit from economy of force advantages while facing the challenge of a modern Chinese army. The question for Moscow has been at what price. The price to return to the negotiating table should not be higher than the benefits expected from resumption of negotiations. The fact is that with or without CFE, the numbers are going down, and cuts will ensure that the limits will remain higher than actual holdings.

And yet should CFE unravel, the Russian military would likely have to focus more on the European front. Most analysts agree that this would prompt the Russian military to rely more heavily on tactical nuclear weapons to defend itself in Europe and would thus complicate any future Western efforts to reduce or limit Russian tactical nuclear weapons either through a U.S.-Russian agreement or some other arms control arrangement. Moreover, should CFE fall apart, it would not be quickly or easily replaced, given the complexity of the regime and heightened sense of uncertainty and growing suspicion that would accompany a collapse of the current arrangements.

In the face of considerable budgetary constraints, likely defense cuts in Europe, and a period of continued uncertainty in European security, the United States and its Allies continue to have a high stake in the future of conventional arms control and confidence-building in Europe. Congress and American officials including military officers may have had limited exposure to conventional arms control and may view the CFE Treaty as irrelevant. However, judging from U.S. military requirements in Europe today in terms of number of troops and equipment, and considering the defense and military cuts announced, there is cause for concern. In addition, with the refocus of U.S. interests further east, Americans could be seen as having overlooked their increased security commitments in Europe in the post–Cold War era with an enlarged NATO. Moreover, the point of CFE has been to ensure that the security of Europe would keep U.S. military requirements at low levels in Europe so as to be able to face greater demands elsewhere. In reality, the collapse of the CFE regime could result in greater demands on American security commitments in Europe. So the argument for the U.S. Government is to avoid a situation in which expanded NATO security commitments create additional military requirements at a time when the U.S. military can ill afford to support an increase to respond to European crises.

It is, to a large extent, thanks to the CFE Treaty that the United States was able to bolster its security commitments in Europe with minimal forces while it committed itself to significant wars in Iraq and Afghanistan. In fact, new NATO members in the past few years have pressed the United States and other Allies to devise contingency plans and conduct exercises for their territorial defense in the event of a threat from Russia. In the absence of legal constraints on Russian forces, additional requests for U.S. infrastructure on the territory of the newest Allies could very well increase.

In addition, the CFE Treaty is the main building block of an integrated European security architecture, which has allowed Europe to become a less militarized security environment and has offered transparency and force limitations through clear rules of the game, enabling former enemies to keep suspicions in check. It guarantees predictability and transparency and ensures a Europe at peace and undivided, thus avoiding a resurgence of European security within spheres of influence—NATO versus Russian spheres.

What to Do? It is clear that the status quo on the CFE Treaty cannot be sustained. Continued Russian suspension will ultimately lead to the treaty regime's complete collapse. While the way ahead seems uncertain, Russia must be part of any long-term solution. As it stands, the original CFE regime is slowly fading away with the suspension of information exchanges and onsite inspections. The ratification of the adapted CFE Treaty would seem to be off the agenda.

The prospects for negotiating a new treaty seem rather bleak. Yet there are still some interests on all sides to keep it on the table—but for how long?

Looking ahead, there are apparently two possible options: a concerted effort to save the regime by building on the relevant parts in today's security environment with some legally binding commitments (a new CFE Treaty), along with politically binding aspects; or preparation for a soft landing based on politically binding elements, thus transitioning to a different regime based essentially on the Organization for Security and Co-operation in Europe (OSCE) Vienna Document.

The real issue, however, lies in the fact that Russian complaints concerning the CFE Treaty are much broader than the treaty itself. It stems from post–Cold War wounded pride and frustration over deals that a weak Russian government accepted in the 1990s, but which Putin's Russia called into question. Russian authorities have registered their uneasiness with various developments, which they consider to be inimical to Russian interests, unfair, and unfavorable to Russian development. This included U.S. plans for missile defense and further NATO enlargement, and was significantly complicated by Russian military action against Georgia and recognition of Abkhazia and South Ossetia in 2008.

In fact, following its decision to suspend the CFE Treaty, Russia tabled a draft European Security Treaty aimed at rearranging the European security system, including proposed mechanisms for crisis consultations and collective security. However, Medvedev's pan-European treaty concept did not address the current arms control regime. That said, it clearly indicated Moscow's vision in terms of European security, and the fact that whatever may be negotiated in the future, this vision would have to be accommodated if Russia is to be part of European security debates and mechanisms. One might wonder whether Medvedev's proposal can be co-opted toward preserving and updating the CFE Treaty. Given the complexity of the CFE regime, its future would require a specific and distinct approach, but this paper argues that negotiations over CFE would greatly benefit from a parallel dialogue on a common pan-European security vision.

Russia's desire for an equal seat at the European security table must be built on the existing system of European security structures and channeled through approaches that further integrate, not divide Europe. Russian leaders may well want to create leverage to have some of their CFE Treaty complaints addressed, rather than abandon the treaty entirely. The Russian government will not be of a single view on this issue, but the one person to convince and the only player able to reverse the Russian position is and will remain Putin.

Given today's financial constraints including ongoing and upcoming defense cuts, the general trend will remain one of reductions on all sides. It would seem timely and appropriate to look at real numbers rather than virtual ones. Indeed, the relatively uncoordinated European defense cuts, including substantial decreases by Central and Eastern European countries and projected American manpower reductions, could negatively affect reassurance among Allies as well as the relationship with Russia. The United States recently announced force posture revisions for U.S. European Command (USEUCOM) to be implemented in 2015. The United States will apparently retain two Brigade Combat Teams vice three from the current deployment level. These teams will likely be complemented by missile defenses on land (Poland and Romania).[20]

In light of upcoming cuts, USEUCOM might be uniquely well placed to engage a process to review real holdings as opposed to virtual ones according to the CFE Treaty limits, and thus assist in reenergizing interest in negotiations with Russia. USEUCOM would also be in a position to look at the possible implications that missile defense deployment and enhancements to support training and installations in Central and Eastern Europe might have regarding limits, if any, according to the CFE Treaty. The limits that NATO committed to in terms of forward deployment of forces in the context of the NATO-Russia Founding Act of 1997, which aimed at constraining both nuclear deployments and permanently stationing additional substantial combat forces on the former Warsaw Pact territories, would have to be kept in mind. This could be an opportunity to address one of the longstanding Russian concerns over the precise definition of *substantial combat forces*. It would also have to be part of a multilateral process, given the lack of consensus among the Allies on this issue, but it could be informed by USEUCOM in the context of upcoming cuts and serve as an incentive to get Moscow interested in reengaging seriously on a treaty for CFE.

A new CFE Treaty would effectively allow for ongoing and announced defense budgetary cuts and focus this CFE Treaty on existing holdings as opposed to agreed limits, given that all parties have significantly reduced their conventional forces in Europe. It would also aim at reassuring all parties, including Russia, in the face of growing suspicions (notably after 4 years of CFE Treaty suspension). The biggest challenge would likely be the development of a successor to the "flank regime," which under the CFE Treaty provided for higher equipment levels in the flank regions (both north and south) of Russian territory, as well as additional inspections and information exchange on equipment in the flanks. Given the uncertainties and tensions, notably in the Caucasus over the past decade, a successor to the flank regime would require years to finalize. This would still be a better option than a likely regionalization of Europe that would ensue should the CFE regime be allowed to collapse, with additional suspicions within the European security environment given the upcoming cuts and modernization efforts. The alternative to a new CFE Treaty would rely on the Vienna Document and likely lead to regionally based talks, as developed in the context of the Dayton Accords, in postconflict areas through CSBMs adapted to specific regional contexts.

It should be clear, however, that salvaging the CFE Treaty will not happen without addressing some of the key European security dilemmas raised by the Russians—be it NATO enlargement, missile defense, and issues relating to the Russian so-called near abroad. These issues cannot be addressed through CFE Treaty negotiations alone or any other arms control negotiations. Similarly, it should be well understood that arms control still has a role to play in U.S. and NATO relations with Russia. While it is true that arms control was developed as a tool for managing risks in an adversarial security relationship, the recent return to arms control debates to engage with Russia may not necessarily imply a return to an adversarial relationship. It may just be an indication that the relationship between Russia and the West is in a state of flux that is best characterized as "unfinished business." The possibility of a surprise attack has been successfully eliminated, largely by Cold War arms control efforts. Furthermore, war in today's environment, given NATO and Russian military postures, has certainly become largely impossible on either side, at least in the short to mid term. That said, despite earlier efforts at cooperative security, the idea of a genuine security community including Russia has failed.

The temptation to resort to arms control, therefore, is rooted in a desire to close the loop and assist in moving toward a genuine security community. In this particular context, the role of arms control seems to have evolved from mitigating the consequences of military confrontation during the Cold War to an important tool in today's environment in support of a deteriorating political relationship between Russia and the West.[21] The hope of arms control is to avoid a slide back to military confrontation and to maintain the ultimate goal of cooperation toward an inclusive security community in Europe.

As long as the transformation of relations between NATO and Russia, as well as between the United States and Russia, remains incomplete, and while it is still unclear whether this transition will lead toward a true and inclusive security community, arms control will remain relevant. It will provide all parties with security reassurances by restraining or prohibiting specific military options. It will provide transparency on military activities on all sides and some mechanisms to address security concerns. That said, arms control has never excluded the use of more cooperative frameworks in the context of multilateral negotiations.

Damage Control on Missile Defense Cooperation

Potential cooperation between the United States and Russia on missile defense, as well as between NATO and Russia, has been considered by many experts and officials on all sides as a potential "game changer" in Moscow's relations with Washington and Brussels.[22] It has also been a major irritant in these relationships over the years. Nonetheless, at the latest NATO summit in November 2010 in Lisbon, Medvedev agreed with his NATO counterparts in the NRC to explore NATO-Russia missile defense cooperation. The objective has been to create a more stable, secure Europe and NATO through U.S. missile defense deployments defined in President Obama's European Phased Adaptive Approach (EPAA) to defend Europe from growing ballistic missile threats from the Middle East. From 2011 to 2020 under EPAA, U.S. missile defense systems will be deployed in Poland, Romania, Spain, and Turkey as well as in international waters around Europe.

For some, this development held the prospect of changing missile defense from a major irritant in East-West relations to a subject of cooperation both bilaterally and multilaterally.[23] The fact is that it would be one of the few instances whereby Allies and Russia would consider a joint response to common challenges and help the parties get past their misgivings about their respective roles in European security.

Since November 2010, discussions have taken place in both NATO-Russian and U.S.-Russian channels, with significant exchanges of information on practical issues relating to missile defense, building on prior discussion notably in the context of cooperation in theater missile defense. However, signals and political statements from Russian authorities in autumn 2011 were far less encouraging. Already in early May 2011, the Russian foreign ministry reacted dourly to the U.S.-Romania agreement on a site for basing U.S. SM-3 missile interceptors in 2015. Senior Russian officials subsequently insisted that Moscow requires "legally binding guarantees" that U.S. and NATO missile defenses would not target Russian strategic ballistic missiles. The Russian request for legal guarantees betrays a need for reassurance facing lack of trust and confidence in the offer of cooperation extended by the United States and NATO.

Cooperation in missile defense is marred by various structural challenges. It is rooted in a challenging historical debate that has surrounded the very idea of missile defense over the past 20 years. Cooperation is also challenged by the diverging threat perceptions emanating from Moscow, Washington, and even Brussels. Finally, it is challenging from the perspective of a significant technological gap in terms of capabilities and the sense of vulnerability carefully hidden behind an aggressive rhetoric in Moscow. These structural challenges will make it difficult to develop cooperation in this field irrespective of the potential that such cooperation might hold in terms of changing the European security game between East and West once and for all.

That said it is worth remembering (especially in light of the results of the 2012 Russian presidential elections) that in June 2007, Putin proposed to George W. Bush at a G-8 summit in Germany that their countries cooperate and jointly use the Soviet-era early warning radar station in

Gabala, Azerbaijan, leased by Moscow. Moscow requested, however, that Washington abandon its plans to build a radar station in the Czech Republic. Moreover, Putin suggested that Washington should rely on its Aegis missile defense system rather than deploy ground-based interceptors in Poland. A month later, at the so-called Lobster Summit at the Bush family compound in Maine, Putin added that Moscow would also agree to sharing data from another early warning radar station located in Armavir, Russia, and suggested establishing joint information-sharing centers. However, Putin insisted that cooperation with Russia would require that the United States abandon its missile defense plans for Poland and the Czech Republic, which top Russian military and political leaders regarded as potentially threatening to their own nuclear forces. It is, therefore, not surprising that 2 years later, when the Obama administration retired plans to deploy ground-based interceptors in Poland and X-band radar in the Czech Republic, opting instead for the EPAA, this move was welcomed by Moscow, leading to the November 2010 NATO summit in Lisbon, with positive statements on possible cooperation between Russia and NATO and Russia and the United States. However, substantive cooperation has yet to materialize.

Diverging Threat Perceptions. In the past 2 years, U.S. officials bilaterally as much as multilaterally have tried to assure Moscow that EPAA will neither target Russian nuclear strategic forces nor be capable of intercepting sophisticated Russian intercontinental ballistic missiles (ICBMs). EPAA is intended to counter missile threats essentially from Iran, which has made significant progress in its efforts to develop its own ballistic-missile program and uranium-enriched capacities.

Despite regular briefings and serious transparency efforts on the part of the United States and its Allies, a number of Russian leaders and experts insist that Iran's missile program poses no credible threat to the United States, Europe, or Russia, and that Russia has no evidence that Teheran is pursuing nuclear weapons capable of being mounted on these missiles. Russian generals, for their part, do not deny that the "potential threat from the south" really exists, but they consider the threat vague; therefore it does not require any urgent countermeasures because neither Iran nor North Korea actually have delivery systems with sufficient range, and many years will be required to acquire such long-range missiles. Their development and testing will be noticed sufficiently early to react to in due course. Of course, this is a dubious argument given that logically, it would seem pointless to wait for a first ICBM to be developed prior to working on a ballistic missile defense (BMD) system to address the situation when it is already too late, especially when there is today an option to anticipate and preempt this development. The Russian argument, however, is not based on logic but on psychology, and the fear of uncertainty. It is clear that there is more to Russian resistance than meets the eye.

According to knowledgeable Russian experts, the real issue for the Russian generals seems to be that the threat to Russia is not coming from Iran but from EPAA, as they are convinced that this system is aimed at Russian ICBMs, and no serious, logical argument seems to change their position. The fear is often rooted in a perceived threat years down the road rather than in existing challenges and capabilities. On the basis of the information provided to the Russian side, but also on the basis of American budgetary planning and congressional hearings also available to the public at large, Moscow accepts the fact that the EPAA in its present configuration and scope matches the Iranian-type threat rather than the Russian strategic deterrent capability, even when the Russian nuclear arsenal will be reduced to the level required by New START. The Russian side acknowledges that countering the Russian capability would require a far more complex BMD system with thousands of interceptors and probably dozens of interceptor launch sites. Nevertheless, the U.S. system may yet evolve in the future under different administrations with different threat perceptions, and American technology is so advanced that the evolution of the U.S. system remains potentially destabilizing for Russia, according to the generals.[24]

In terms of threat perceptions, the Russian "sectoral approach" to missile defense cooperation was most telling. At the 2010 Lisbon Summit, Medvedev offered a proposal for establishing a sectoral BMD cooperation framework. At a news conference following the NRC meeting of heads of state and government, he stated, "We proposed building a sector-based missile defense system. Our conditions are equality, transparency, technological involvement and responsibility for particular tasks." This suggests that the Russian sector would include some Baltic states and Poland in Central and Eastern Europe. These countries were quick to respond—rightly—that as Allies they intended to be defended by NATO and certainly not by Russia.

The offer betrays that the Russian side seems much more concerned about a NATO system defending the Baltic states in Central and Eastern Europe than it is of Iran's nuclear capabilities. It is a clear indication of nervousness on the part of Russian generals to have a system in this region that might ultimately develop a capability over Russia and its missiles—a geopolitical issue—that is to say, a structural challenge that will be hard to overcome because geographical realities hardly change. Russia's sectoral BMD proposal stems from fears about the launch sites in Poland as well as in the Baltic region and northern Europe in general. Continued reassurance through transparency and dialogue over time will be the only way to address this structural challenge to missile defense cooperation.

Destabilizing Capability and Technology Gap. The real question regarding the sectoral approach should have been whether Russia actually would have had the technical capability to protect the very region it intended to assign to its sector from missile threats. Again relying on

Russian experts' publication,[25] the Daryal-type early warning radar in Gabala was Russia's first proposed contribution to a cooperative framework. It should be noted that the radar would be a valuable asset as it covers the southern areas where the missile threat might originate. The radar could be integrated into a joint BMD system. However, one should underline that, for reasons of its original design and specifications, it would not be able to guide American or Russian interceptors to their targets. Moreover, the agreement between Russia and Azerbaijan on Gabala is coming to an end (2013) and might close the window of opportunity in terms of NATO-Russia cooperation before it even opens.

Theoretically, Russia could also contribute the Don-2N multirole surveillance station near Moscow. The station, which has a 360-degree view, would have to be upgraded before it could be integrated into a joint BMD system. That said, the Don-2N is part of Russia's national missile defense system that covers the area around its capital, and it is unclear whether Moscow would be prepared to share this vital facility for its own national security to a joint BMD system. In any event, this is the extent of the Russian capability that might contribute to EPAA.[26]

When it comes to the Voronezh-DM early warning radar in Armavir, which many have considered as a potential contribution to a proposed joint BMD system, it is unclear whether this capability would be necessary or could even be used. Indeed, the edge of the Armavir radar's range runs along the middle of the European continent from east to west. In the east, the line runs from Armavir to the Black Sea coast of the Caucasus on to Turkey, Syria, and further south. In other words, the range of the radar reaches to part of the Middle East, the Mediterranean, and almost the whole of North Africa but does not include Iran, which is shielded from the radar by the Caucasus Mountains.[27]

Another Voronezh-DM radar station now being built near Kaliningrad is even less useful since it is directed toward Europe. In fact, Russia's threats to station missiles near Kaliningrad or to start building intermediate-range missiles again if the United States stations elements of its BMD system in Europe run counter to the idea of cooperation in missile defense. Thus, all these radars could potentially be used as elements of a missile attack warning system but not as an actual missile defense system. Russia's contribution in terms of interceptors and guidance radars is to date nonexistent. So when the Russian military claimed that it could take care of a sector in a joint BMD system, and insisted that Russia could defend such a sector without actually stationing any of the interceptors or guidance radars on that territory, they actually discredited themselves in the eyes of knowledgeable experts within Russia itself.[28]

Moreover, what little is known from official documents and open sources about Russian missile defense efforts suggests that the available financing in this area is woefully inadequate in Russia. More information is available on the missile defense capability of the advanced S-500 surface-to-air missile (SAM) system under development, but it is unclear when that system will be ready and how many units the Russian defense industry will realistically be able to deliver, given that Russia is still struggling with delivery of the less complex S-400 (SA-21) SAM system. In the end, it is important to realize that while discussing potential cooperation in missile defense, it is unclear exactly what Russia could contribute in terms of capabilities to the EPAA regime besides two early warning radars.[29]

Finally, it should be noted that the expectation that this cooperation might lead to some technology transfer has proven to be wishful thinking on Russia's part. The technological gap between Moscow and Washington does not help in terms of stability and security in Europe. Technically, Russia is concerned about the future modernization, sophistication, and potential increase in numbers of U.S. interceptors based in Europe. It is also fearful of the quality of sensors to be put in place in Europe and on U.S. ships, which could have the capability to intercept Russian ICBMs at some stage even if the U.S. missile defense systems in place in Europe today and those planned for 2020 do not have the technical capability or boost velocity on interceptors to intercept a Russian ICBM headed from Russia toward the United States.

The reality is that active missile defense cooperation as proposed by either side will *not* happen between Russia and the United States. Both NATO and the United States have moved forward with the first phase of EPAA and will continue to fully protect Europe from ballistic missile threats with or without Russia's consent. Russia will continue to fight publicly and diplomatically against NATO and American resolve to deploy missile defenses in Europe. The United States has been transparent and open to cooperation with Russia, as Russia has similar threats from the Middle East and maintains sophisticated radars and active missile defense systems deployed against them. However, Washington will not accept any limitations or restrictions on the development or deployment of U.S. missile defenses. Where does this leave missile defense cooperation in the runup to the NATO summit in Chicago, in May 2012, as Putin returns to power and looks for concessions from President Obama?

A Possible Way Forward. It remains in the best national interest of both Russia and the United States to maintain military situational awareness on ballistic missile threats to Europe from the Middle East. Joint military awareness would provide security and stability for Europe, Russia, and the United States. Transparency among Russia, the United States, and NATO on missile defenses in Europe should remain, but this does not necessarily imply sharing classified information or cooperating on respective missile defense *systems*.

A political commitment not to target each other with interceptors in a NATO-Russia Declaration on missile defense cooperation at the upcoming Chicago Summit could help and might include some practical elements of cooperation, including the sharing of early warning information. There is indeed scope to build on what was originally a proposal from Putin. The Pentagon has been interested in gaining access to data from Russian radars located northwest of Iran, such as the Gabala radar, that could provide useful tracking information to NATO on an Iranian missile launch toward Europe. In March 2011, Secretary of Defense Robert Gates indicated that it would be possible to set up a joint data fusion center, allowing greater transparency concerning our missile defense plans and exercises and conducting a joint analysis to determine areas of future cooperation. While the NRC could support this type of cooperation, bilateral discussions between Moscow and Washington will drive the process.

Under the U.S. proposal, joint data fusion centers would allow Russian and NATO officers to have simultaneous access to missile launch data from sensors in NATO countries and Russia, giving both sides a full real-time picture of potential threats, according to U.S. officials. Media reports indicate that these centers would combine data from fixed and mobile radar sites as well as from satellites.[30] Establishing centers for data exchange and building a common operating picture would allow for shared training in operations and for other cooperative arrangements, which would give Russia a greater sense of comfort. In the NATO-Russia context, joint data fusion centers could mirror the Cooperative Airspace Initiative in the NRC framework, which delivered two centers for data exchange and support to military exercises.

Ultimately, for missile defense cooperation to take roots, it is in the interest of NATO and the United States to reassure Moscow and to offer transparency with some avenues for cooperation. However, one should refrain from ambitious game-changer rhetoric, given the lack of broad European security dialogue and of trust and confidence. While missile defense theoretically has the potential of becoming a game changer, the United States, NATO, and Russia are still far from that possibility given the unfinished business of European security. While a genuine cooperative and strategic relationship should remain the ultimate goal, the priority should be on less ambitious but more feasible projects, especially in an election year both in the United States and in Russia.

Many have stated that the future of missile defense cooperation with Russia would be a major determining factor in Russia's willingness to consider further reductions regarding non-strategic nuclear weapons. Generally speaking, too much hinges on progress in missile defense cooperation in current debates in U.S.-Russia and NATO-Russia frameworks. In reality, when it comes to missile defense, we should aim solely at surveillance data exchange, providing interoperability of early warning systems, and conducting joint exercises. Faced with a dilemma as to whether one should use missile defense cooperation to improve relations with Russia (the game-changer argument) or first improve the relations before considering serious missile defense cooperation between systems, this paper favors the latter approach.

A Broad Security Dialogue: Addressing the Unfinished Business

To deal with specific requirements to follow on New START and overcome the stalemate on the CFE Treaty, while considering the potential for cooperation in terms of missile defense, one cannot rely on existing bilateral and multilateral frameworks as they stand today. One of the key conclusions of the past 20 years of cooperative efforts between the United States and Russia and within the NATO-Russia framework should be that the sum of positive developments and cooperative projects—albeit significant—has never amounted to a strategic partnership with Russia.

Ongoing negotiations regarding the future mix of conventional, nuclear, and missile defense forces in Europe, and regarding the uncertain future of the CFE Treaty, as well as ongoing discussions over cooperation in missile defense, are all intertwined in terms of their inherent potential to anchor the reset policy with Russia. These issues are also linked by their ability to derail the challenging process of engagement. The ultimate goal should be to help Russia feel sufficiently secure so Moscow can consider discussing (bilaterally and multilaterally) limitations on its nonstrategic nuclear weapons while acknowledging its conventional inferiority. This will not happen without a genuine attempt to engage in a broad security dialogue, and to urgently reassure Moscow by addressing its own longstanding and well-documented concerns regarding European security. In the absence of such a broad engagement, positive developments on either file may occur, but they will remain tactical positive steps, falling short in terms of strategically (re)setting the agenda in the long run.

Developing the Process to Engage Russia

The vertical structure of power in Russia and the fact that its president does not seem to use independent, external sources of advice does not favor change and actually hampers "new thinking" from developing. Moreover, the limited Russian independent advice and expertise used by defense/security officials does not easily assist the Kremlin in technical discussions such as missile defense debates or CFE Treaty negotiations. Access to Russian experts in the area of missile defense seems limited to the inner circles of the General Staff, given the powerful lobby of Russian generals in this field. In fact, it would seem that on missile defense, the General Staff is formulating the Russian position. However, military advice is not enough. A political-military approach is necessary.

As Putin returns to the presidency in 2012, it will be essential to engage and seek political solutions at the top. There may be more hope in Putin as a deal breaker than in missile defense as a game changer. However, for Putin to trust any cooperative scheme with Western partners, the context will have to change. Of course, it will change should oil prices drop to the point of getting Russia on its knees. Beyond such a scenario, there will have to be a broad framework to discuss European security issues, including conventional force nuclear matters, NATO enlargement, and zero-sum approaches in the so-called near abroad with Russia. In parallel with this broad political dialogue, there will have to be some reassuring messages manifest through concrete activities, be they in the context of Afghanistan, in terms of military exercises and planning, in terms of transparency or innovative ideas about "smart defense," and regarding possible joint installations, such as data exchange centers. All these steps will have to be presented to Putin himself in another attempt to build trust and in the hope of giving him alternative thinking to address thorny issues.

Nevertheless, the real question for the United States and NATO is whether there is real interest in a "deal" with Russia, as the new Russian president in May 2012 will most likely be looking for one. Following the lukewarm reception to the Medvedev initiative among Allies, new ideas will have to come from the West. It is not entirely clear whether the United States and NATO truly need something from Russia in today's security environment, and it is even less clear that consensus can be developed on that basis within the U.S. Congress in an election year, or within today's Alliance. In that sense, the timing of Putin's return to the presidency will be an issue, as it is unlikely that the Russian president himself will be looking for a renewed engagement with Washington prior to the November 2012 elections in the United States. Some positive steps and signals may be sent through an NRC Declaration in May 2012, however, should this remain an option.

Ultimately, 2012 will be a time to reflect and consider a new approach in the form of a comprehensive political-military framework to deal with the unfinished business of the post–Cold War. In engaging with Russia, and while aiming eventually at genuine cooperation in areas such as missile defense, one should remember the significance of the unfinished business in Europe, and the fundamental differences between Russia and Allies on threat perceptions, European security architecture, and the general lack of trust and confidence. We are facing essentially an "interim period" toward strategic partnership with Russia—assuming progress. In this interim period, tools such as arms control, confidence-building measures, and reassurance through various programs will be critical. While it does not preclude serious cooperative activities as demonstrated in various areas such as NATO-Russia cooperative airspace, genuine cooperation cannot be assumed.

Moreover, bilateral and multilateral attempts to develop a genuine and inclusive security community in Europe will be crucial to accompany upcoming defense cuts in 2012 and to assist in delivering on today's security priorities and defense commitments outside Europe. A high-level political-military process aimed at addressing the unfinished business of Europe, notably the challenging relations with Russia, should develop a broad security dialogue in support of presidential efforts, especially in Washington and Moscow. It should also develop international efforts mostly from NATO and the OSCE, also drawing on independent expertise from the community of security experts and recent "Track Two" efforts to ultimately assist the Kremlin and the White House in setting the agenda post-2012. High-level coordination between bilateral and multilateral efforts will be as important as bringing together political and military efforts.

Developing the Agenda to Engage Russia

In the aftermath of the Russo-Georgian war, the United States and NATO have addressed the challenges of a difficult relationship with Russia by essentially reassuring the Central and Eastern European Allies while reaching out to Russia in general terms through cooperative activities. The challenge with this approach has been that measures taken by NATO and the United States to reassure Central and Eastern European Allies have usually been interpreted by Moscow as antagonistic, triggering Russian rhetorical and military responses including exercises and the maintenance of nonstrategic nuclear weapons to counter their conventional inferiority. Similarly, measures to build confidence with Russia and any attempt to mutually reduce nonstrategic nuclear weapons systems have often been perceived in Central and Eastern Europe generally (although the views there are not monolithic) as a weakening resolve on the part of the Alliance to use its capabilities, and ultimately a weakening of the NATO Article 5 commitment.[31]

For its part, Moscow reacted on numerous occasions to what it has consistently perceived as threatening moves against it. In 2009, Russia conducted military exercises (Ladoga and Zapad) near the Baltic states, which foresaw a simulated nuclear attack on Poland. Moreover, when Warsaw decided to host U.S. ground-based interceptors as part of the Bush administration's Third Site missile defense program, Moscow responded by threatening to target Russian nuclear systems in Kaliningrad—a threat reiterated at the end of 2011, given the lack of progress on potential cooperation with Russia in the area of missile defense. Moreover, the weakness of Russian conventional forces has led to a "first use" nuclear doctrine. Finally, in 2010, Russian military doctrine reiterated language previously used against NATO's expansion and its global projection capability as threats against the Russian Federation.[32]

The U.S. reset policy, like NATO outreach cooperative efforts, has fallen short of reassuring Russia despite the rhetoric of the 2010 Lisbon Summit and the so-called strategic partnership between NATO and Russia. In today's European security context, trust and confidence are elusive. In addition to a broad security dialogue involving political and military high-level engagement, a specific set of measures to build confidence with a far-reaching bilateral and multilateral cooperative program needs to be developed on the basis of today's security agenda to reassure Russia. Tangible results of concrete measures toward this end will take time and proceed through incremental steps to build confidence. Such a program of confidence-building should focus on five main areas of particular relevance to the United States and the Allies in today's European security environment that should have resonance in Moscow.

Operational Cooperation. One of the most successful approaches to build confidence and trust with partner countries has proved to be operational cooperation. Unfortunately, operational cooperation with the Russian military in NATO-led operations has been limited. Negative experiences inherited from the Balkan wars, notably with the 1999 Pristina airport episode, have not helped in building trust. Renewed efforts at developing interoperability between allied and Russian units should be a must if the NATO-Russia relationship is to take root and develop. Considering recent interest in counterpiracy cooperation, and building on previous cooperation in the area of search and rescue at sea, as well as limited cooperation in the context of NATO's Article 5 Operation *Active Endeavor*, positive naval cooperation with Russia could pave the way for developing a joint naval task force, which could be the basis for developing interoperability between the Allies and Russia.

Similarly, developing interoperability on the basis of successful cooperative efforts in counterterrorism between air force units from Poland, Turkey, and Russia in the framework of the NATO-Russia Council Cooperative Airspace Initiative could assist in reassuring Russia about allied intentions and offer greater transparency regarding NATO activities in the Baltic Sea region. From June 6 to 10, 2011, NATO and Russian fighter aircraft took part in counterterrorism exercise Vigilant Skies 2011, a joint demonstration of the NRC Cooperative Airspace Initiative (CAI). This initiative was designed to prevent civilian aircraft from being used in a terrorist attack, such as occurred on September 11, by sharing information on movements in NATO and Russian airspace and by coordinating interceptions of renegade aircraft. This new airspace security system provides a shared NATO-Russia radar picture of air traffic and allows early warning of suspicious air activities through commonly agreed procedures. The new system has two coordination centers—in Warsaw and Moscow—and local coordination sites in Kaliningrad, Rostov-on-Don, Murmansk (Russia), Warsaw (Poland), Bodø (Norway), and Ankara (Turkey). This was the first counterterrorism exercise held between NATO and the Russian Federation and remains a major milestone in terms of operational capability of the CAI system and of operational cooperation with Russia.

Finally, enhanced cooperation in the context of Afghanistan, greater transparency with regard to American and allied intentions, and activities post-2014 International Security Assistance Force (ISAF) transition would also offer serious prospects for genuine cooperation with Russia and regional cooperation more broadly. So far, cooperation with Russia regarding Afghanistan has focused on counternarcotic efforts, transit through the northern route for cargo shipments in support of ISAF to and from Afghanistan, and a trust fund established in support of helicopter maintenance. This has been punctual and limited to specific areas of cooperation, often on a commercial basis. There is, however, limited political discussion with Russia (or other countries in the area) on possible regional cooperation beyond the 2014 transition to Afghan security forces and withdrawal of ISAF troops, and little talk about NATO's enduring partnership with Afghanistan beyond 2014 with countries in the region, including Russia. This could offer some cooperative opportunities toward future stability and security through a dialogue involving Russia, Central Asia, Pakistan, and possibly India, China, and Iran although the challenge of developing such a dialogue is obvious.

Transparency on Contingency Planning and Exercising. Despite earlier efforts at cooperative security, and acknowledging that for the time being the idea of a genuine security community including Russia has failed, it is imperative to ensure, in the interim period, transparency efforts on Article 5 contingency planning on the NATO side and corresponding planning on the Russian side through maximum transparency and prior warning when exercising such contingency plans. In the absence of a working CFE regime, transparency and dialogue in the NRC could assist and complement any other mechanisms foreseen in the Vienna Document.

Dialogue on Deterrence and Transparency—Safety Measures Regarding Tactical Nuclear Weapons. While the Alliance is conducting its DDPR, dialogue is urgently required if the Allies are truly committed to engaging Russia on negotiations over the reductions of tactical nuclear weapons. Given today's European security environment and Russian conventional inferiority, Moscow is unlikely to see any interest in reducing its nonstrategic nuclear weapons without a broader effort—a security dialogue with a meaningful set of reassurances.

While some discussions in the DDPR context are meant for agreement within the Alliance (at 28) and therefore restricted to members, Allies would benefit from greater transparency and openness toward Russia in this regard. Indeed, readiness level, delivery systems, weapons-life extension and dual-capable aircraft issues, deployment options, and command

and control issues are essentially internal allied considerations. Other elements of the debate should lead to discussions with Moscow, notably regarding transparency and safety measures. Over time, these discussions would be particularly useful in the context of possible reductions on the NATO side, through consolidation sites, for instance. Reductions, while discussed bilaterally, may also be part of an overall multilateral arms control approach whereby Moscow may be persuaded to consolidate its own sites and agree to develop reciprocal transparency and safety measures.

Ultimately, the Allies may be faced with reductions of nonstrategic nuclear weapons for internal politics and budgetary constraints without benefiting from any reciprocal reductions on the Russian side. This would be counterproductive for the Alliance, whereas, should NATO finally engage with Russia in this debate, there may be parallel efforts at transparency measures, relocation of sites away from NATO-Russia borders, and mutual reductions that are safe, secure, effective, and credible. This was certainly the sense given in the 2010 NATO Strategic Concept, which stated, "In any future reductions, our aim should be to seek Russian agreement to increase transparency of its nuclear weapons in Europe and relocate these weapons away from the territory of NATO's members."

Such a dialogue with Russia would have to feed into a comprehensive framework including both a more traditional bilateral arms control treaty format, and a multilateral track on the basis of the OSCE Vienna Document, as well as the NRC. Taken together, these measures could create the conditions for negotiations of nonstrategic nuclear weapons reductions.

Extension of Smart Defense Approaches and Projects. The economic recession and fiscal austerity, accompanied by a reduced sense of strategic threat, have led most Allies to reduce their defense budgets significantly, while Russia will most likely struggle with its defense reform and modernization efforts in the face of widespread corruption and budgetary constraints, irrespective of its defense budget commitments announced in 2011. Moreover, the United States announced force posture revisions of USEUCOM to be implemented in 2015. In the face of defense cuts, including substantial reductions in Central and Eastern Europe, the hope on the Alliance side is that smart defense will offset some of these cuts: "Examples of smart defense might include establishing regional multinational forces, sharing regional equipment and facilities, pooling funds for enablers such as the C-17 consortium, creating some niche capabilities and specializing."[33] While the Alliance may retain capabilities and funding for top priority missions, some of these missions may require and integrate partner capabilities. There may be scope for developing such a construct to include Russian contributions.

Russia has developed bilateral armament cooperation with certain Allies, which has prompted some uneasiness within the Alliance, in particular over the French sale of the *Mistral-*

class amphibious ship to Russia. That said, such cooperation may turn into future opportunities in terms of operational cooperation between NATO and Russia, and could open new avenues for pooling and sharing with Russian companies. Prior negotiations over cargo aircraft on a commercial basis have already taken place involving allied and Russian authorities. While there is considerable resistance within the United States for any cooperative efforts that might lead to technology transfer, this should not preclude some cooperation in support of smart defense.

Joint Installations. Countries of Central and Eastern Europe have consistently called for allied presence on their soil for reassurance, while NATO was limited in its forward deployment options, given promises made in the context of the NATO-Russia Founding Act of 1997, which constrained both nuclear deployments and permanent stationing of any "significant combat" forces on the territories of new Allies and former Warsaw Pact members. That said, NATO responded to requests for air policing of the air space of Allies who could not afford to do so themselves. The Alliance also assisted in developing training centers such as the Cooperative Cyber Defence Centre of Excellence, located in Estonia. NATO decisions, however, always took into consideration the risk of antagonizing Russian political and military leaders regarding any attempt to move military installations closer to their borders.

Providing similar incentives to Russia, developing joint infrastructure might help reassure Moscow of NATO's intentions. There are various options that could be discussed and developed in the framework of the NRC, building on the successful CAI, which is an interesting precedent that could provide for the development of future additional joint centers with Russia to exchange data and to assist in future cooperative security programs. This could be considered in the context of missile defense cooperation should this project develop positively in the future.

In sum, a program of transparency and confidence-building in the five areas mentioned previously would offer concrete steps toward enhancing trust and provide real substance to a political-military dialogue between Russia and the West. Such a broad dialogue at multilateral and bilateral levels would help address the current issues confronting NATO and the Allies in a concrete and pragmatic manner. It would deal head-on with the unfinished business of the Cold War and provide the necessary conditions of cooperative security to ultimately lead to a genuine European security community.

Conclusion

In light of ongoing and upcoming defense cuts in the Euro-Atlantic community, which will continue to affect the Allies nationally and NATO multilaterally, synergies between bilateral efforts and multilateral cooperation may have to become more prominent to ensure that the unfinished business of post–Cold War European security is not allowed to drift. The U.S. commitment to Europe and Russia is fundamental to the ability of international organizations to pursue their respective transformation agendas. Moreover, the ability of multilateral arenas to address security issues will also be challenged by the complexity of addressing priorities in the face of fiscal constraints. Russia may not be a priority for all Allies, and consensus within NATO on how to best engage with Moscow will remain challenging. For its part, Russia has long favored the NRC as a consultative mechanism even in the midst of severe crisis and deterioration of dialogue between the Allies and Russia. However, the NATO-Russia Strategic Partnership envisaged in the 1997 Founding Act and the 2002 Rome Declaration never fully materialized despite the fact that both NATO and Russia are strategic players who cannot ignore each other in defining and addressing security challenges in and around Europe. Today's declaratory policy hardly matches the facts on the ground, and the rules of the game remain blurred with actors at times borrowing from the cooperative set of tools while resorting to adversarial negotiation tactics when politically expedient. While the ultimate goal may still be to build a strategic partnership based on broad cooperation and win-win solutions, it will be a bumpy and long road ahead. While the end result is not assured, the rules of the game between NATO and Russia have to be refined. The game should be one of building confidence and providing reassurances if there is to be any hope of getting back to the broad cooperative agenda envisioned in the founding documents mentioned herein.

In that context, U.S.-Russia bilateral relations and the future of the reset policy will remain a significant building block to secure a broad cooperative agenda with Russia on the long run. The relationship with Moscow cannot be allowed to drift. A serious effort at engaging with Russia and addressing the unfinished business of post–Cold War European security with its well-known contentious issues will be required to develop an inclusive security community, which in turn will be a sine qua non condition for facing no less challenging issues looming on the horizon, and relating to regions beyond Europe, such as the Caucasus, Middle East, North Africa, Central Asia, and High North. In the absence of a cooperative security environment in Europe, regional issues may lead to serious confrontations over strategic resources and diminishing defense resources and thus come to challenge the very European security that institutions such as NATO have guaranteed for decades. Creative thinking and consolidation of efforts to come to terms with this unfinished business of the post–Cold War era in European security is urgent.

Notes

[1] Julianne Smith, *The NATO-Russia Relationship: Defining Moment or Déjà vu?* (Washington, DC: Center for Strategic and International Studies, 2008).

[2] George Robertson, "A New Quality in the NATO-Russia Relationship," *International Affairs* 48, no. 1 (2002), 32–37.

[3] North Atlantic Treaty Organization (NATO), *Strategic Concept for the Defense and Security of the Members of the North Atlantic Treaty Organization*, 2010, available at <www.nato.int/lisbon2010/strategic-concept-2010-eng.pdf>; and NATO, *NATO-Russia Council Joint Statement*, November 20, 2010, available at <www.nato.int/cps/en/natolive/news_68871.htm>.

[4] NATO, *NATO and Russia: A New Beginning*, speech by NATO Secretary-General Anders Fogh Rasmussen at the Carnegie Endowment, Brussels, September 18, 2009, available at <www.nato.int/cps/en/natolive/opinions_57640.htm>.

[5] NATO, *Statement by the NATO Secretary-General on Missile Defense*, November 23, 2011, available at <www.nato.int/cps/en/natolive/news_81198.htm>.

[6] NATO, *Founding Act on Mutual Relations, Cooperation and Security between NATO and the Russian Federation*, signed in Paris, May 27,1997, available at <www.nato.int/cps/en/natolive/official_texts_25468.htm>.

[7] NATO, *NATO-Russia Relations: A New Quality*, May 28, 2002, available at <www.nato.int/cps/en/natolive/official_texts_19572.htm>.

[8] NATO, *NATO and Russia*.

[9] Ben Lombardi, *Strategic Assessment—Russia: Strategic Culture and Foreign Policy*, DRDC CORA Technical Memorandum 2009-016, April 2009.

[10] NATO, *NATO and Russia*.

[11] NATO, *Lisbon Summit Declaration*, November 20, 2010, available at <www.nato.int/cps/en/natolive/official_texts_68828.htm>.

[12] Secretary of State Hillary Clinton had put forward five principles regarding the nuclear agenda: 1) as long as nuclear weapons exist, NATO will remain a nuclear alliance; 2) as a nuclear alliance, widely sharing nuclear risks and responsibilities is fundamental; 3) the broader goal of the Alliance must be to reduce the number and role of nuclear weapons and recognize that NATO has already dramatically reduced its reliance on nuclear weapons; 4) the Alliance must broaden deterrence against 21st-century threats including missile defense, strengthening Article 5 training and exercises, and drafting additional contingency plans to counter new threats; and 5) in any future reductions, NATO's aim should be to seek Russian agreement to increase transparency on nonstrategic nuclear weapons in Europe, relocate them away from the territory of NATO members, and include nonstrategic nuclear weapons in the next round of U.S.-Russia arms control discussions alongside strategic and nondeployed nuclear weapons.

[13] Oliver Meier, *NATO Revises Nuclear Policy*, Arms Control Association, December 2010, available at <www.armscontrol.org/print/4590>.

[14] Lukasz Kulesa, *Roma Locuta, Causa Finita? The Nuclear Posture Review and the Future of U.S. Nuclear Weapons in Europe*, Carnegie Endowment for International Peace, April 27, 2010, available

at <www.carnegieendowment.org/2010/04/27/roma-locuta-causa-finita-nuclear-posture-review-and-future-of-u.s.-nuclear-weapons-in-europe/avk>.

[15] Meier, *NATO Revises Nuclear Policy*, 3.

[16] Steven Pifer, *The United States, NATO's Strategic Concept, and Nuclear Issues*, Nuclear Policy Paper, No. 6, 2011, Arms Control Association, British American Security Information Council, Institute for Peace Research and Security Policy at the University of Hamburg, 5.

[17] Ibid.

[18] Oliver Meier, *Next Steps in Arms Control: Nuclear Weapons, Missile Defense and NATO*, presentation at the Arms Control Association, Washington, DC, November 18, 2010.

[19] Tom Z. Collina, *The Conventional Armed Forces in Europe (CFE) Treaty and the Adapted CFE Treaty at a Glance*, Arms Control Association, available at <www.armscontrol.org/print/4458>.

[20] Hans Binnendijk and Catherine McArdle Kelleher, *NATO Reassurance and Nuclear Reductions: Creating the Conditions*, Transatlantic Current 2 (Washington, DC: NDU Press, 2011), 7, available at <www.ndu.edu/press/lib/pdf/trans-current/Trans-Current-2.pdf>.

[21] Andrei Zagorski, "Strengths and Weaknesses of the Current Arms Control Regimes and CSBMs," forthcoming book chapter.

[22] Simon Saradzhyan, *Breaking the Stalemate of Collective Insecurity in Europe* (Cambridge, MA: Belfer Center for Science and International Affairs, Harvard Kennedy School, June 2011).

[23] Steven Pifer, *Obama, Medvedev and Missile Defense*, May 20, 2011, available at <www.brookings.edu/opinions/2011/0521_arms_control_pifer.aspx?p=1>.

[24] Aleksandr Stukalin, *Missile Defense: Old Problem, No New Solution*, Moscow Defense Brief, February 2001, available at <www.mdb.cast.ru/mdb/2-2011/item4/article1/?form=print>.

[25] Ibid.

[26] Ibid.

[27] Ibid.

[28] Ibid.

[29] Ibid.

[30] Tom Z. Collina, *Russia Makes New Proposal on Missile Defense*, Arms Control Association, April 2011, available at <www.armscontrol.org/print/4780>.

[31] Binnendijk and Kelleher.

[32] Carnegie Endowment, *The Military Doctrine of the Russian Federation*, February 5, 2010, accessed at <www.carnegieendownment.org/files/2010russia_military_doctrine.pdf>.

[33] Binnendijk and Kelleher, 7.

About the Author

Dr. Isabelle François is a Distinguished Senior Visiting Research Fellow in the Center for Transatlantic Security Studies, Institute for National Strategic Studies, at the National Defense University. She served previously at North Atlantic Treaty Organization (NATO) Headquarters as Head of Euro-Atlantic Integration and Partnership. From 1998 to 2011, she held various positions on the NATO International Staff, including Director of NATO Information Office in Moscow (2004–2009). She received the Medal of Excellence from the NATO Secretary-General in 2007 for a significant public diplomacy event—the 2006 NATO-Russia Rally—organized in the Russian Federation. She has worked within the Alliance on a range of issues dealing with NATO partnerships and outreach policy. Before joining the Alliance, she served at the Department of National Defence (DND) from 1993 to 1998 in the Policy Group, both within the NATO Directorate (1996–1998) and Directorate of Strategic Analysis (1993–1996), where she published extensively on defense issues related to Africa and Europe. She then took a more operational assignment as part of the team in charge of drafting the 1994 Canadian Defense White Paper. Dr. François holds a Law Degree from Université de Paris XII (France) and is a graduate of Carleton University (MA) in Ottawa, Ontario, and Université de Montréal (Ph.D.) in Québec.

Center for Transatlantic Security Studies

AMBASSADOR ROBERT HUNTER
Director

MR. LAWRENCE CHALMER
Deputy Director

MR. MARK DUCASSE
Research Fellow, Contractor

MR. ULF HAEUSSLER
Visiting Senior Research Fellow

DR. ISABELLE FRANÇOIS
Distinguished Research Fellow, Contractor

MS. AMANDA LOWE
Program Assistant

MS. KATHRYN MOSS
Outreach Coordinator, Contractor

MS. ALICE NING
Program Manager, Contractor

MR. STEFANO SANTAMATO
Senior Research Fellow, Contractor

MR. BRETT SWANEY
Program Assistant

Nonresident Subject Matter Experts

DR. CHARLES BARRY
Senior Research Fellow, Contractor

MR. MICHAEL DURKEE
Distinguished Research Fellow, Contractor

MR. PETER FLORY
Distinguished Research Fellow, Contractor

DR. RICHARD KUGLER
Distinguished Research Fellow, Contractor

MR. JACK SEGAL
Distinguished Research Fellow, Contractor

MR. STAN SLOAN
Senior Research Fellow, Contractor

MR. BRUCE WEINROD
Distinguished Research Fellow, Contractor

For a complete list of INSS researchers and staff, please visit www.ndu.edu/inss/index.cfm.